O9-BTJ-890

To _____

From _____

Happy Grandmothering

When a child is born, so is a grandmother.

. ITALIAN PROVERB.

When a Child Is Born, So Is a Grandmother

Illustrated by
Mary Engelbreit

**Andrews McMeel
Publishing**®

Kansas City · Sydney · London

Andrews McMeel Publishing, LLC
an Andrews McMeel Universal company
1130 Walnut Street, Kansas City, Missouri 64106

www.andrewsmcmeel.com
www.maryengelbreit.com

. is a registered trademark of
Mary Engelbreit Enterprises, Inc.

14 15 16 17 18 TWP 18 17 16 15 14

ISBN: 978-0-7407-0204-4

Written by Jan Miller Girando

When a Child Is Born, So Is a Grandmother

A grandchild!
The news puts your life in a tizzy.
You've just been promoted!
You'd better get busy.

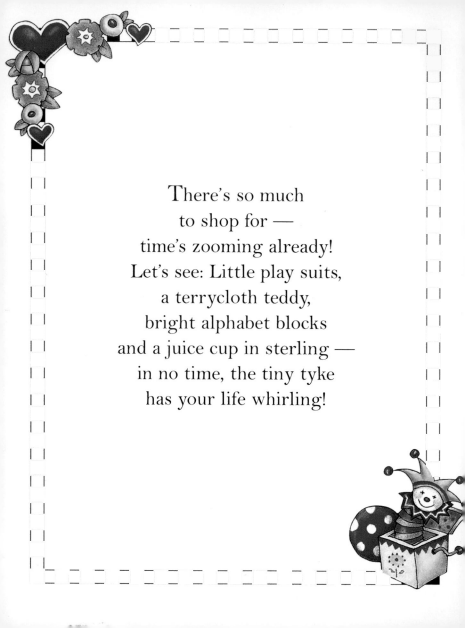

There's so much
to shop for —
time's zooming already!
Let's see: Little play suits,
a terrycloth teddy,
bright alphabet blocks
and a juice cup in sterling —
in no time, the tiny tyke
has your life whirling!

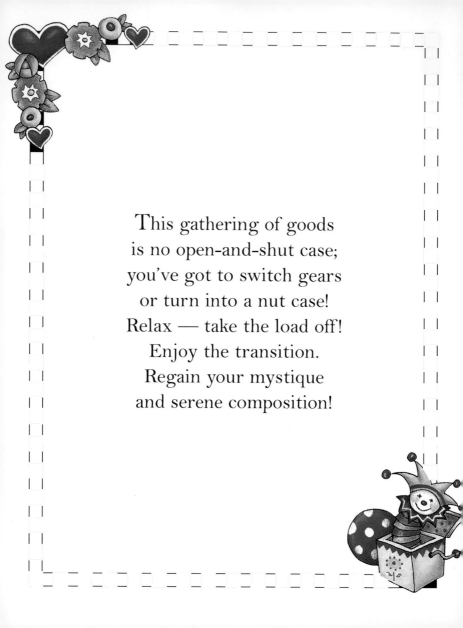

This gathering of goods
is no open-and-shut case;
you've got to switch gears
or turn into a nut case!
Relax — take the load off!
Enjoy the transition.
Regain your mystique
and serene composition!

A grandma with flair
and a sense of direction,
you'll focus on style —
it's more fun than perfection!

THE QUEEN MOTHER

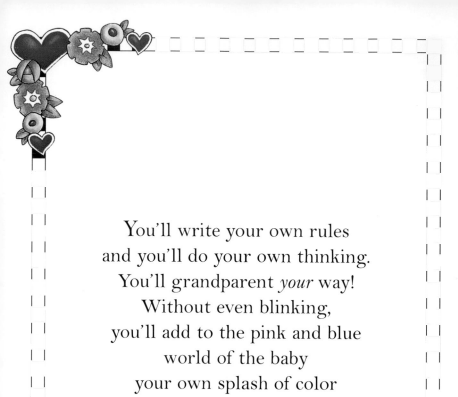

You'll write your own rules
and you'll do your own thinking.
You'll grandparent *your* way!
Without even blinking,
you'll add to the pink and blue
world of the baby
your own splash of color
(or just a dash, maybe).

You're launching your legacy
with innovation
and boldly defining
the next generation!

No need to wear aprons,
make pies or bake cookies —
that timeworn scenario's
strictly for rookies!

Select from the past
the traditions you treasure,
then give them your own
special flair for good measure.

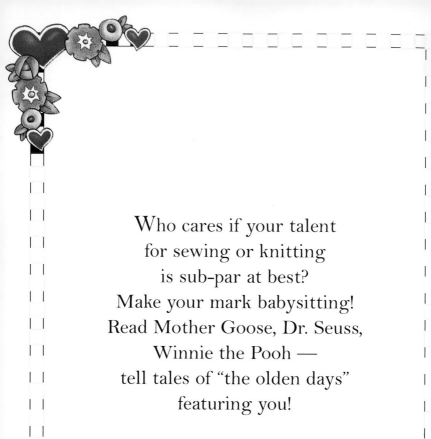

Who cares if your talent
for sewing or knitting
is sub-par at best?
Make your mark babysitting!
Read Mother Goose, Dr. Seuss,
Winnie the Pooh —
tell tales of "the olden days"
featuring you!

You're bound to excel
in advanced coochy-cooing;
before long, you'll know
when the storm clouds are brewing!
If fussing transpires,
no need for a stand-off —
find Mommy or Daddy
and relish the hand-off!

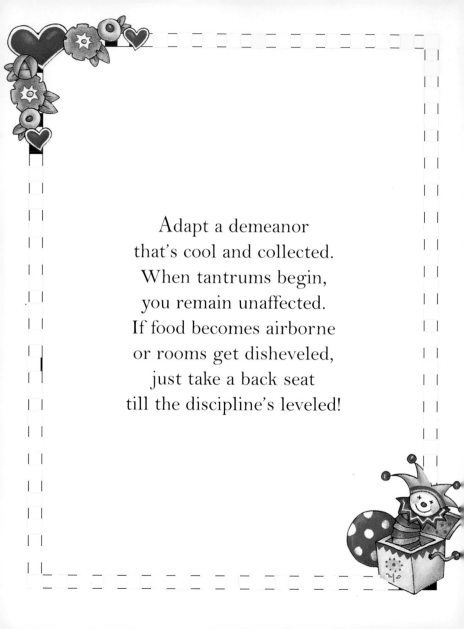

Adapt a demeanor
that's cool and collected.
When tantrums begin,
you remain unaffected.
If food becomes airborne
or rooms get disheveled,
just take a back seat
till the discipline's leveled!

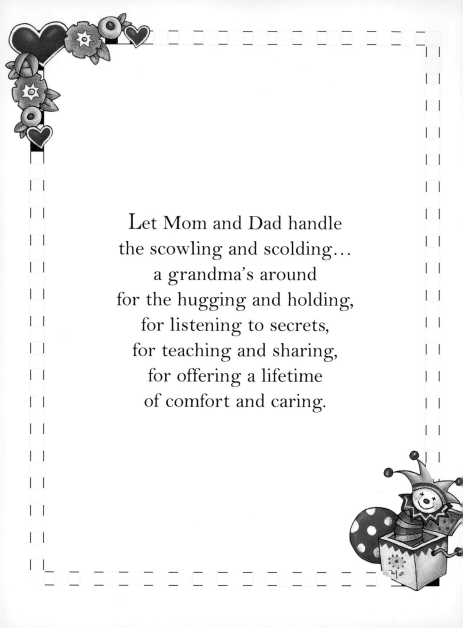

Let Mom and Dad handle
the scowling and scolding…
a grandma's around
for the hugging and holding,
for listening to secrets,
for teaching and sharing,
for offering a lifetime
of comfort and caring.

A loyal supporter
of every endeavor,
you'll share a close bond
with your grandchild forever.
A beautiful future's
unfolding for you —
when a grandchild is born,
a grandmother is, too.